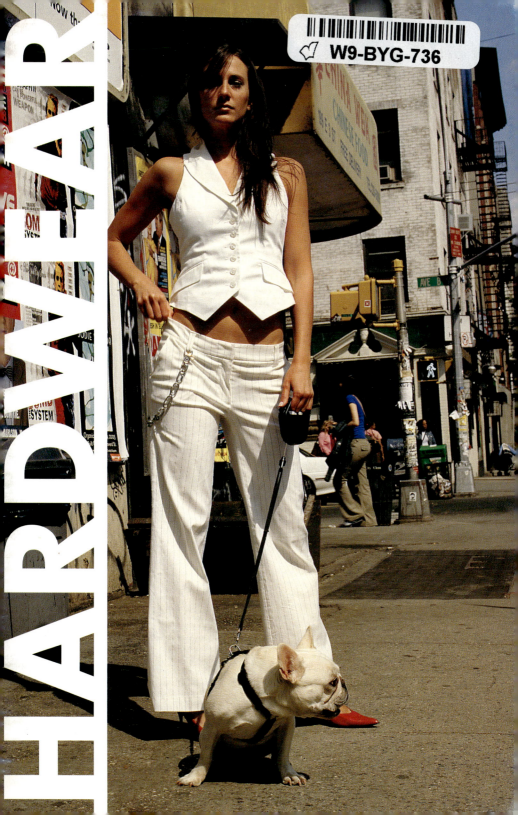

HARDWEAR

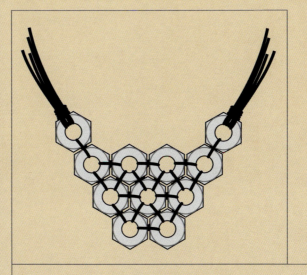

JEWELRY FROM A TOOLBOX

Hannah Rogge

Photographs by
Marianne Rafter

STC Craft | A Melanie Falick Book
STEWART, TABORI & CHANG NEW YORK

Project Manager: Christine Gardner
Editor: Melanie Falick
Designer: Roger Gorman and Carl Williamson
Production: Kim Tyner

Library of Congress Cataloging-in-Publication Data:

Rogge, Hannah.
  Hardwear: jewelry from a toolbox/Hannah Rogge;
  photographs by Marianne Rafter–1st ed.
      p. cm.
  ISBN 1–58479–480–1(hardcover)
1. Jewelry making. I. Title.

TT212.R64 2006
745.594'2–dc22
                                          2005020810

Published in 2006 by Stewart, Tabori & Chang
An imprint of Harry N. Abrams, Inc.

The text of this book was composed in Futura.

Printed and bound in China
10 9 8 7 6 5 4 3 2 1

HNA ■■■■■
harry n. abrams, inc.
a subsidiary of La Martinière Groupe

115 West 18th Street
New York, NY 10011
www.hnabooks.com

To Robie and Fred (my parents, not my long-lost goldfish),
for extending support and encouragement to me and my friends...
and, truthfully, for both being very cool.

CONTENTS

INTRODUCTION

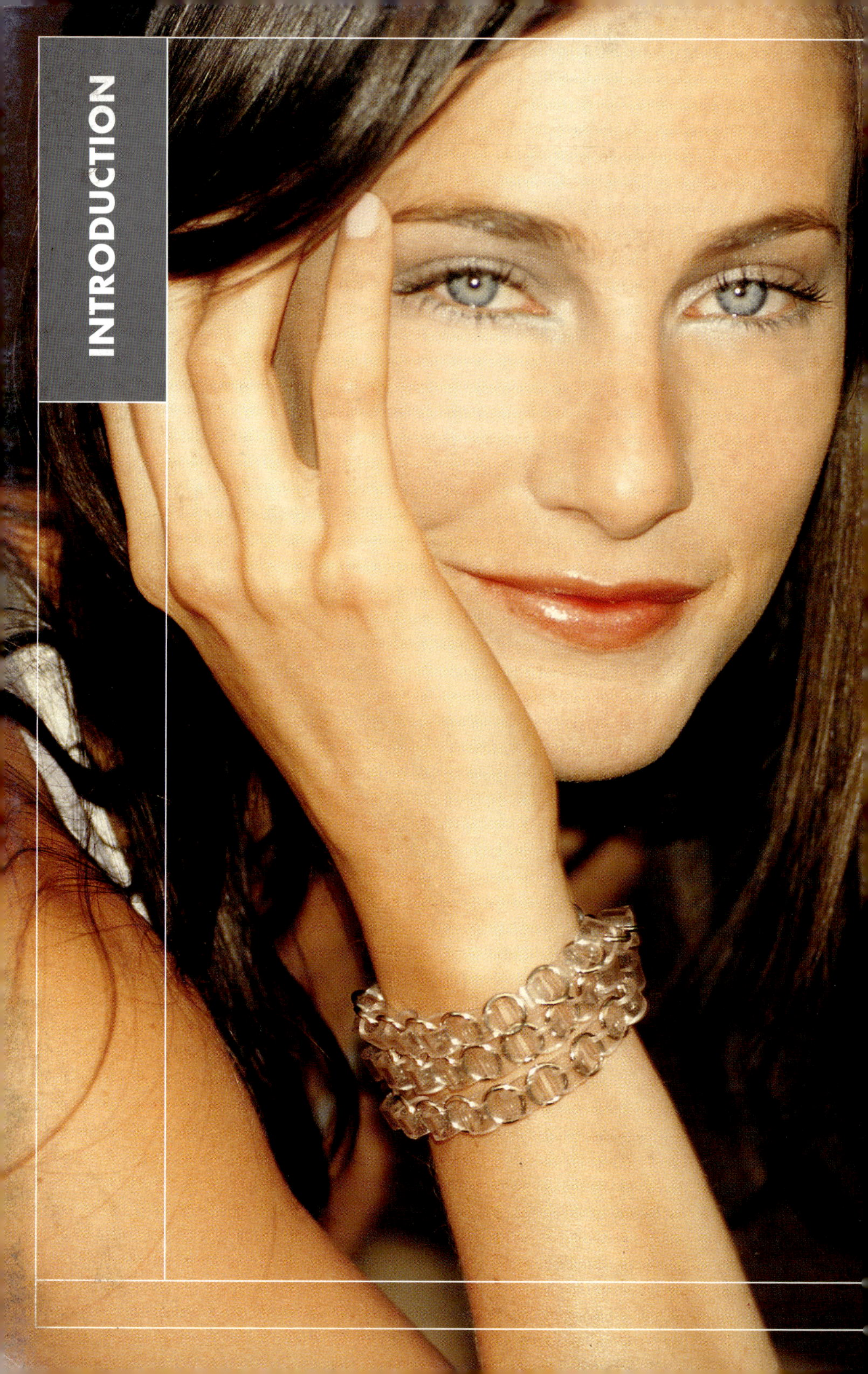

A few years ago, I was in a hardware store creative problem-solving. Well, ok—I guess that's what most everyone is doing at a hardware store, since we are usually there desperate to fix some household disaster. But during that particular visit I was feeling a different kind of desperation: I needed holiday gifts for my friends, and shopping for them is never an easy task. My friends are creative, interested in innovative design, and have great taste. And for that kind of taste, I had little money.

I wandered the aisles thinking about the simple geometry of the parts and pieces in front of me: hexagons (nuts), circles (washers), squares (L-brackets), ovals (quick links), and rectangles (hinges). And then the answer came to me: I could probably make interesting jewelry from this hardware. My first project was a pair of hex nut earrings for my friend Frances. I was thinking of the nuts as beads, but then had to figure out how to attach them to each other. I experimented with different strings and knots, eventually settling on common materials found in a bead store: nylon-coated wire and crimping beads (which are often used in tandem). The earrings were a hit. Frances loved them when I gave them to her and wears them to this day. (They are, in fact, her "lucky" earrings—she says things go well for her when she wears them.) My friend Emily didn't have her ears pierced at the time, so for her I turned the earring design into a necklace, which you will find on page 84. The necklace got a lot of compliments and I began to get requests for more. One style alone was not enough to keep my creative juices flowing, so I went back to the hardware store and began to experiment with other ideas and materials, eventually expanding my "collection" to include bracelets, belts, zipper pulls, charms, and even hair clips. Now, when I am at my day job at a custom design and fabrication studio (we design and build exhibits, visual merchandising displays, and animated windows), I cannot help but think of ways to turn the greasy hardware on my worktable into elegant accessories.

For me, the contradiction implicit in making jewelry out of hardware is perfect because I love breaking boundaries and challenging the "norm." The idea is high/low. Jewelry is "high," meaning fancy, beautiful, elegant—an unnecessary luxury. Hardware is "low," meaning regular, dirty, and practical. Hardware is traditionally masculine and jewelry is traditionally feminine, but when the two are combined, the result is somehow androgynous and adaptable. I've enjoyed seeing my friends (male and female) wearing my jewelry dressed up and down in elegant clothing, corporate suits, and casual jeans.

In this book, you will find illustrated, step-by-step instructions for making twenty-four of my most popular pieces. At the end of the book is a glossary of all of the materials used in the projects. While most of the supplies are stocked at hardware stores, a few items used to finish the jewelry (like findings and clasps) are sold at bead and craft stores. Wherever you are, I hope you are inspired to think about objects in an untraditional manner, challenging the ideas of assumption . . . and proving that elegance is determined not by money, but by style.

ATTENTION!

There is always something to point out before you start any project using supplies from a hardware store. This time it's about zinc. Most common pieces of sliver-colored hardware are coated in zinc. Although zinc is a compound used in many everyday items, it is not a conventional choice for jewelry because it can darken or change color when exposed to moisture (such as water or sweat). Personally, I enjoy this discoloration because it shows the natural aging of the hardware. Some people, however, don't like the change in color or have skin that is sensitive to zinc. To avoid any difficulties, here are two options:

• Spray both sides of the zinc hardware with clear coat spray paint (in either glossy or matte finish, depending upon your preference) before you make the jewelry. The protective coating will prevent both discoloration and direct contact between the zinc and the skin. Clear coat spray paint is sold in most hardware stores.

• Buy stainless-steel hardware. If your local hardware store doesn't stock it, visit the online sources listed on page 132.

Hardware lends itself to basic geometric shapes. These earrings are elegant for just that reason. Their simplicity makes them easy to wear every day while their length and shiny surface make them dramatic enough for evening wear. Washers have a front side (which is a little more rounded at the edges) and a back side. Although the difference is subtle, the jewelry will have a more professional, finished look if all the washers face in the same direction. You can also substitute hex nuts for washers or combine hex nuts with washers to create earrings with different looks.

TOOLBOX

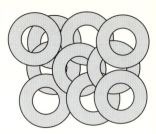

**TEN #8 FLAT SAE
FINISHING WASHERS**

**TWO FRENCH EARRING
WIRES**

**TWO SMALL (⅛)
JUMP RINGS**

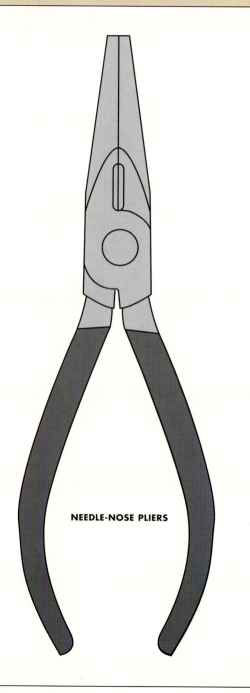

NEEDLE-NOSE PLIERS

**TEN LARGE (1·⁴/₁₀)
JUMP RINGS**

WASHER CHAIN EARRINGS   **12**

1 Open a small jump ring by holding one side of the ring with your fingers while twisting the other side away with the needle-nose pliers.

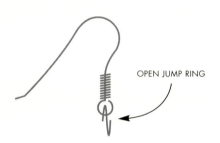

OPEN JUMP RING

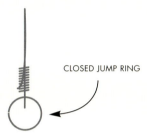

CLOSED JUMP RING

2 Slip the closed circle of a French earring wire through the open small jump ring.

3 Twist the edges of the jump ring back together (with your fingers and the pliers) so the ends touch.

4 Open a large jump ring by twisting one side away from the other side with the pliers.

5 Slip the open large jump ring through the closed small jump ring on the earring wire. Put a small washer through the open large jump ring.

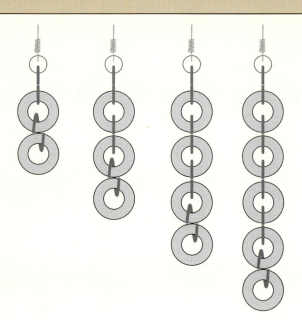

6 Twist the ends of the jump ring together. Twist open another large jump ring and put it through the washer on the earring. Add washers in this manner until you have attached five.

7 Repeat all steps to make a second earring.

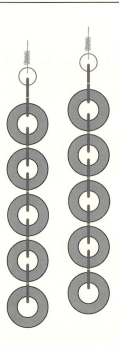

A strip of malleable red rubber contrasts with hard, shiny washers in this fun bracelet. The shape and different sizes of the washers make any pattern, no matter how calculated or random, look interesting.

1/16"-THICK RED RUBBER SHEET PACKING (FOR WASHERS AND GASKETS)

FLEXIBLE MEASURING TAPE OR STRIP OF SCRAP PAPER (AT LEAST 9" x 1.5")

TWO SMALL (1/6) JUMP RINGS

15mm LOBSTER CLASP

SEVEN SMALL #8 FLAT SAE WASHERS

THREE 1/4" MEDIUM FLAT WASHERS

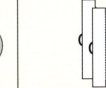

TWO 30mm CHOKER CLAMPS

ONE YARD EMBROIDERY FLOSS, CRAFT TWINE, OR WAXED NYLON MENDING TWINE NO. 3

CRAFT NEEDLE (WITH AN EYE BIG ENOUGH FOR THE TWINE)

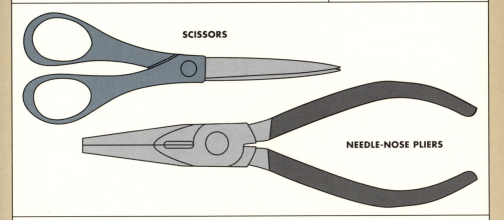

SCISSORS

NEEDLE-NOSE PLIERS

INSTRUCTIONS

1 Using the measuring tape or strip of scrap paper, measure around the wrist to determine the desired length of the bracelet. Note that a clamp will be attached to each end of the bracelet, adding slightly to the length you measure.

2 Measure the exact height of the choker clamp; this will be the width of your bracelet. Cut a strip of rubber to the length and width just measured.

CUT

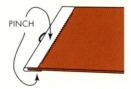

PINCH

3 Slip a choker clamp onto either short end of the rubber. With a pair of needle-nose pliers, squeeze the flat parts of the choker clamp together so they grab the rubber. Repeat with the second choker clamp on the opposite end of the rubber.

4 Open a small jump ring by holding one side of the ring with your fingers while twisting the other side away with the needle-nose pliers.

5 Slip the jump ring through the loop on one of the attached choker clamps. Thread the lobster clasp onto the jump ring and twist the jump ring closed using your fingers to steady one side and the pliers to twist the other side. Twist open another jump ring, slip it through the loop on the choker clamp, and twist to close as before.

6 Thread the embroidery floss or twine onto the craft needle, and tie a knot at the end.

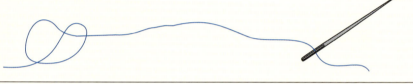

7 Choose one side of the bracelet to be the top. Place a medium washer, rounded surface up, on the top of the bracelet in the desired position.

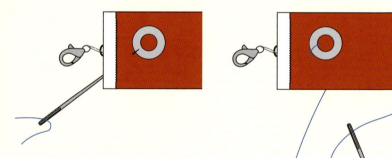

a) Holding the washer in place, bring the threaded needle up through the rubber to the outside of the washer. Pull the thread all the way through until it is stopped by the knot.

b) Push the needle through the rubber close to the inner edge of the washer, directly opposite the first threaded hole made with the needle. The washer should now be stitched to the rubber.

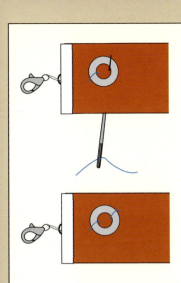

c) Bring the needle back through the rubber at another spot inside of the washer. It is best if this spot is directly across from the end of the first stitch.

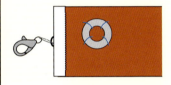

d) Stitch back through the rubber on the outside of the washer as before.

e) Stitch the washer down with two more stitches, creating an X pattern.

BACK VIEW

f) Secure the stitches by tying a knot at the end of the string as it comes out from the bottom. Do this by making a loop and pulling the end through. Cut the end of the string close to the knot without cutting the knot.

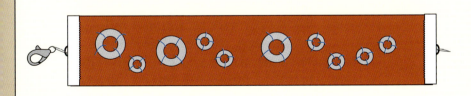

8 Continue to place washers onto the rubber, stitching them down in the desired design.

METAL CIRCLES NECKLACE

This is probably my favorite piece to give as a present because it is simple to make and matches various styles. Once you understand how it is constructed, the design can be applied to bracelets, necklaces, and earrings. Pay attention to the direction of the washers as you put them together (be sure the rounded edges are up) so the end result has a consistent finish. For variety, try changing the size of the washers and the color of leather or rope used to string them together. You can also substitute hex nuts for the washers.

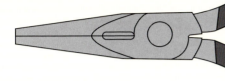

NEEDLE-NOSE PLIERS

**4.5mm
FOLDOVER CORD END**

**TWO SMALL (⅛)
JUMP RINGS**

**7mm SPRING
RING CLOSURE**

**TWENTY-ONE ¼" MEDIUM
FLAT WASHERS**

**36" RUBBER CORD, LEATHER, OR
BLACK ROPE (SIZE 16 OR ³⁄₃₂" DIAMETER)**

METAL CIRCLES NECKLACE

1 Close a small jump ring by holding one side with your fingers and twisting the ends together with the needle-nose pliers. Thread the jump ring through the 36"-long cord. Bring the ends of the cord together so the jump ring falls to the middle.

2 Hold a washer next to the jump ring. The flat surface of the washer should be facing you so you can see through the hole.

3 Put one end of the cord through the hole, entering from the front.

4 Put the other end of the cord through the hole, entering from the back.

5 Hold the next washer up to the first washer so the thin rims of the washers touch. The second washer should be between the two loose cords. Again, the flat surface should be facing you so you can see through the hole.

6 Thread the cord in front of the first washer through the new washer to the back.

7 Thread the cord in back of the first washer through the new washer to the front. Make sure that the cords do not twist.

8 Repeat Steps 5–7 until you have woven all twenty-one washers together.

9 Hold the two cords together and cut them ¼" from the end of the last washer.

10 Place the ends of both cords into the cord end and fold each side over the cords with pliers. Make sure to squeeze it tight and flat with pliers. (If you wish to make this connection even more secure, add a drop of glue inside the cord end.)

11 Open a small jump ring by using your fingers to hold one side of the jump ring and twisting the other side away with pliers. Thread it through the loop in the cord end.

12 Put the loop of the spring ring through the open jump ring and twist the jump ring shut.

13 To close the necklace, open the spring ring and hook it through the small jump ring at the other end.

Zipper pulls make zippers easy to grab and help to identify a bag or jacket quickly. Like the Metal Circles Necklace, this construction can be adapted to different accessories.

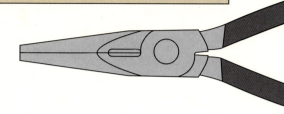

NEEDLE-NOSE PLIERS

LARGE (¹·⁴/₁₀) JUMP RING

SEVEN #8 FLAT SAE WASHERS

10mm (OR BIGGER)
LOBSTER CLASP

12" RUBBER OR LEATHER CORD,
(SIZE 16 OR ³/₃₂" DIAMETER)

INSTRUCTIONS

1 Thread the loop of a lobster clasp through an open large jump ring. Close the large jump ring by twisting the ends together with needle-nose pliers.

2 Thread the cord through the jump ring and bring the ends of the cord together so the jump ring falls to the middle of the cord.

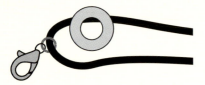

3 Hold a washer next to the jump ring. The large flat surface of the washer should be facing you so you can see through the hole.

4 Put one end of the cord through the hole, entering from the front.

5 Put the other end of the cord through the hole, entering from the back.

6 Hold the next washer up to the first washer so the thin rims of the washers touch. The new washer should be between the two loose cords. The flat surface should be facing you so you can see through the hole.

7 Thread the cord in front of the first washer through the new washer to the back.

8 Thread the cord in back of the first washer through the new washer to the front. Make sure the cords do not twist.

9   Repeat Steps 6–8 until you have woven all seven washers together.

10   Holding the cords together, make a loop and pull the ends through the middle of that loop to make a knot.

11   Cut the cords about ¼" from the end of the knot and clip the lobster clasp to your zipper.

    WASHER ZIPPER PULL

This design started as a choker, but as the proportions incresed it became a belt. This belt has a '70s or '80s feel in its loose fit around the hips. The clasp clips to any part of the belt so one length fits most sizes. If you want to make the belt bigger, add more washers before tying it off. The big metal washers act as flat reflectors, adding a "disco" appeal to any outfit.

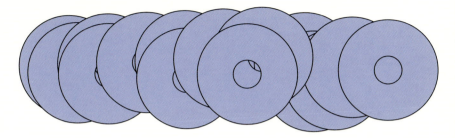

FIFTEEN ½" x 2" ZINC FENDER WASHERS

2½" SWIVEL LANYARD PULL

MATCHES

**TWO 90" PIECES NYLON CORD,
SIZE ⁷⁄₆₄" (NO. 3½)**

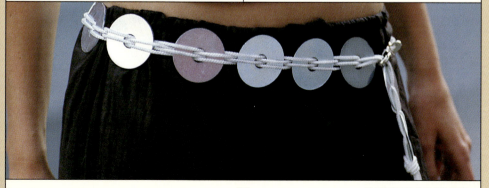

WOVEN WASHER BELT

1 Strike a match and hold it close enough to an end of one rope to melt the tip. Melting the tip will prevent the rope from fraying. Be careful not to put the rope into the flame. Repeat with all four ends of the two pieces of rope.

2 Thread both pieces of rope through the closed end of the swivel lanyard pull. Bring all of the rope ends together so that the swivel lanyard pull falls to the middle of the rope, and four pieces are made from the two.

3 Holding all four pieces together, tie a knot in the rope near the swivel lanyard pull by making a loop and pulling the end through. The swivel lanyard pull should be captured in a loop of rope.

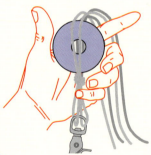

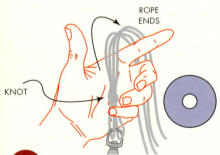

ROPE ENDS

KNOT

4 In one hand, hold the knot so the lanyard pull hangs toward the ground and the rope ends fall over your gripped hand. In the other hand, grab a washer and hold it so you can see though the center hole and the rounded surface (or top) of the washer is facing you.

5 Place the washer above the knot and sandwich it between the rope pieces so two pieces of rope are on the front side of the washer and two pieces of rope are on the back. (In this illustration, the two ropes that begin on the back are shaded in a slightly darker color.)

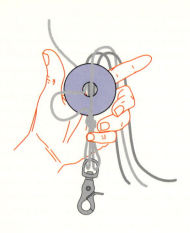

6 Moving from left to right, push the end of the first piece of rope in the front through the center hole of the washer. It is important to make sure the ropes stay in the same order from left to right.

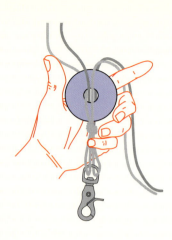

7 Now bring a piece of rope from the back through the center of the washer to the front. This piece should cross though to the right of the first piece that went through the center.

8 Grasp the second front piece of rope and pass it through the hole of the washer to the back. It should cross through to the right of the other two pieces in the center of the washer.

9 Grasp the last piece of rope in the back and cross it through the center hole to the front.

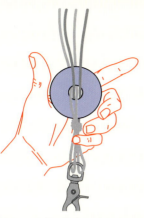

10 Bring all of the rope pieces to the top of the washer. Cross the ropes that are at the back of the washer to the front and the ropes that are at the front of the washer to the back. Make sure that the front and back strings alternate.

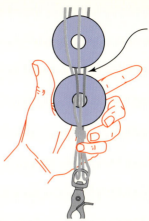

11 Hold the next washer up to the first washer so the thin rims of the washers touch (and the rounded surface is facing you). Put the edge next to the crossed ropes, sandwiching the washer between two pieces of rope in the front and two pieces of rope in the back.

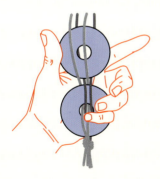

12 As before, weave the front pieces through the washer to the back and the back pieces to the front, alternating the order in which you weave the rope pieces through the washer.

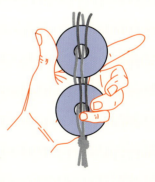

13 Bring all of the rope pieces to the top of the washer. Cross the ropes at the back of the washer to the front and the ropes at the front of the washer to the back. Make sure the front and back ropes alternate.

14 Repeat Steps 12 and 13 until all fifteen washers have been woven into the rope.

15 Holding all of the ropes together, tie a knot at the end of the last washer by making a loop and pulling the ends through.

16 Tighten the knot close to the last washer. To wear the belt, wrap it around your hips and squeeze open the lanyard pull. Clip it onto the rope where it fits best around your hips (most likely between two washers).

This necklace is interesting because it uses neon-colored string in a zigzag pattern, and the design seems to suit the neon color. This pendant is adjustable and can also be made into a pin or a hair clip by gluing it onto different backings.

TOOLBOX

MATCHES

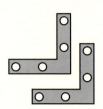

**TWO 1½" x ⅜"
ZINC-PLATED
L-BRACKETS**

GLUE

**72–84" NEON
NYLON ROPE**

INSTRUCTIONS

1 Strike a match and hold it close
enough to an end of the rope to
melt the tip. Melting the end will prevent the rope from fraying. Be careful not to put the rope into the flame.
Repeat on the other end.

CUT

2 Put the two ends of the rope together and cut the loop that is made at the
center, leaving two equal amounts of rope.

3 Strike a match to melt the newly cut tips of the rope. Holding the two pieces
of rope side by side, tie a knot by folding the rope over itself and pulling the
ends through the loop. Make sure this knot is bigger than the holes in the L-bracket.
If the knot is too small, tie another knot on top of the first one.

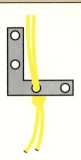

4 If you look closely at the L-bracket, you will see that one surface has slightly rounded edges (this is the top of the bracket) while the opposite surface is completely flat (this is the bottom of the bracket). Holding one of the brackets face up and in the direction of an L, thread both strands of the knotted rope up through the bottom middle hole. Pull the ropes through until you reach the knot.

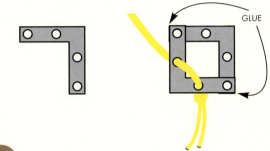

GLUE

5 Thread the end of the ropes down through the hole diagonally to the left.

6 Hold the second bracket like an upside-down L, making sure that the rounded surface is on top. Place behind the first bracket so the corners of the brackets touch, making a square. To keep the brackets from moving, put a small drop of glue at the corners where they touch.

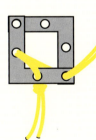

7 Thread the ropes up through the bottom right-hand hole. The ropes should have gone through a hole in each bracket.

8 Thread the ropes down through the upper left-hand hole. The ropes should have gone through a hole in each bracket.

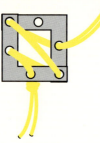

9 Thread the ropes up through the hole in the upper right-hand side of the square.

10 Thread the ropes down through the upper center hole.

11 Thread the ropes up through the lower center hole. This is the same hole you started stringing through.

12 Thread the ropes down through the upper center hole.

13 To wear the necklace, separate the two pieces of rope and put the pendant around your neck. Tie the rope in a bow at the desired length.

This simple, unisex bracelet is easy to customize by wrapping different lengths of wire at various points along the rope. The copper color of the wire contrasts well with the white nylon rope.

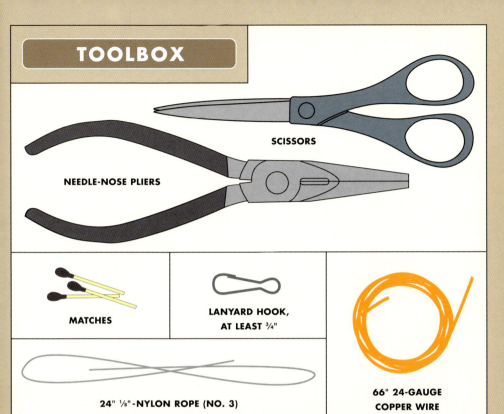

SCISSORS

NEEDLE-NOSE PLIERS

MATCHES

LANYARD HOOK,
AT LEAST ¾"

24" ⅛"-NYLON ROPE (NO. 3)

66" 24-GAUGE
COPPER WIRE

INSTRUCTIONS

1 Using the wire cutters that are in the middle of the needle-nose pliers, cut 48" of the copper wire and set aside.

2 Wrap the nylon rope loosely around the wrist twice (making two complete circles without overlapping) to determine the size of your bracelet. Cut the rope to size. You can also measure the distance around the wrist with a flexible tape measure and double that measurement.

3 Strike a match and hold it close enough to one end of the rope to melt the tip. Melting the end will prevent the rope from fraying. Be careful not to put the rope into the flame. Repeat at the other end of the rope.

4 Thread 1¼" of the rope through the hole of a lanyard hook. There should now be a short and a long side of the rope, as determined by the position of the hook.

5 Fold the short side of the rope over, capturing the hook in a loop. Fold the long side of the rope over so the tips of the rope touch each other. Hold the bracelet together in this position.

6 Bend ¼" of the 48"-wire at a right angle and place it next to the folded rope.

7 Bend the wire around both pieces of rope, about ¼" away from the touching tips. Make sure the end of the wire faces the direction of the tips.

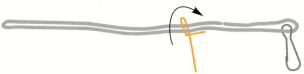

8 Twist the wire around the rope and over the touching tips, covering about 1" of the rope. Continue wrapping the wire around the rope, overlapping the wire within that 1", until you are almost out of wire.

9 Tuck in the end of the wire so no sharp edges protrude. It may be easier to use a pair of needle-nose pliers or to leave a longer end to tuck in.

10 Cut another piece of wire 12" long. Bend ¼" of the wire at a right angle and place it around the two adjacent pieces of rope about 1" away from the end without the hook. Make sure the bent end of the wire faces the longer part of the bracelet. Start wrapping the wire tightly around the rope in the direction of the bent wire end, covering it. Continue wrapping back and forth, covering about ½" of the rope. Be sure to tuck the end of the wire into itself to prevent sharp edges from protruding.

11 Cut another piece of wire 6" long. Bend ¼" of the wire into a right angle, and place it around the rope about ¾" from the last wrapped section. Make sure the bent end of the wire faces the longer part of the bracelet. Wrap the wire tightly around the rope as before, covering ¼" of the rope. Be sure to tuck the end of the wire into itself.

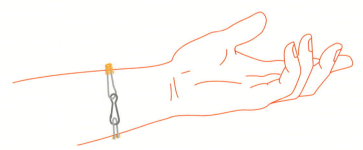

12 To close the bracelet, latch the hook around the loop made by the rope.

These earrings are really simple and the perfect gift for a glam girl, especially when made in neon pink.

TOOLBOX

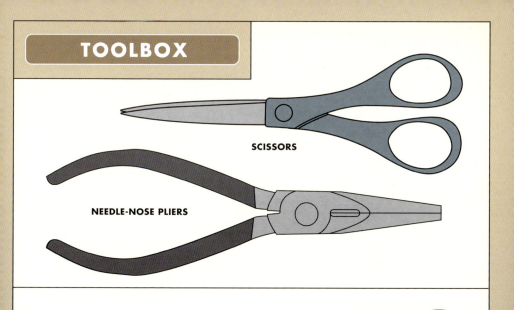

SCISSORS

NEEDLE-NOSE PLIERS

24" NEON NYLON ROPE

TWO FRENCH EARRING WIRES

TWO SMALL (⅙) JUMP RINGS

MATCHES

NEON ROPE EARRINGS

1   Cut two 12" pieces neon nylon rope.

2   Strike a match and hold it close enough to an end of one of the ropes to melt the tip. This will prevent the rope from fraying. Repeat on the remaining three ends of rope.

SIDE VIEW

3   Twist open a small jump ring with a pair of pliers by holding one side with your fingers and twisting the other side with the pliers. Thread the jump ring through the loop of a French earring wire.

4   Twist the jump ring closed.

FRONT VIEW

5   Thread both pieces of rope through the jump ring.

6 Holding all four ends of the rope together, tie a knot in the rope by making a loop and pulling the end through. Pull the knot tight about 1½" from the earring wire.

7 Repeat Steps 3–6 to make a second earring.

This clip is fun because you can recognize the hardware. Pin hinges curve smoothly around a hair clip to create this surprising accessory.

TOOLBOX

MATCHES

80mm FRENCH PONYTAIL BARRETTE

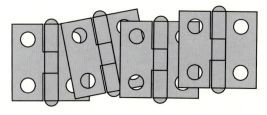

FOUR 1" ZINC-PLATED NON-REMOVABLE PIN HINGES

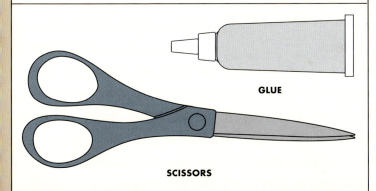

GLUE

SCISSORS

12" NEON NYLON ROPE

INSTRUCTIONS

1 Line up the hinges in a row so the middle spines are vertical and face up.

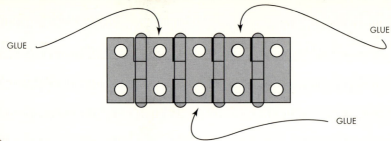

GLUE   GLUE

GLUE

2 Overlap the adjacent sides so the holes align, and glue those pieces to one another. It will be easier if you wait until the glue is almost completely dry (check glue label for drying time).

3 Tie a double knot at the end of the rope by making a loop in the rope and pushing the end through it without tightening. Then, cross the end of the rope around the side of the loop again and through a second time, this time pulling the knot tight.

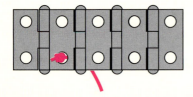

4 From the top (the side where the hinge spines stick up), thread the rope to the back through the bottom left hole of the overlapping hinge sections. Pull the rope all the way through until it stops at the knot. Make sure the knot does not pull through the hole. Cut the short end of the rope close to the knot without cutting the knot.

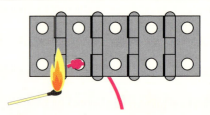

5 Hold a flame up to the end of the knot just close enough to melt the knot together and to prevent the end from fraying.

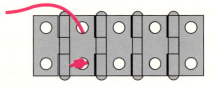

6 Bring the rope up through the other hole in the section.

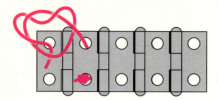

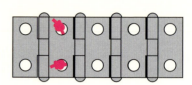

7 Tie another double knot in the rope as in Step 3. Be sure to pull the knot as close to the hole as possible.

8 Cut the rope close to the knot without cutting the knot.

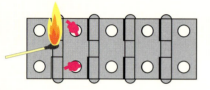

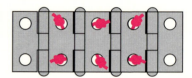

9 Hold a flame up to the end of the knot just close enough to melt the knot together and to prevent the end from fraying.

10 Repeat Steps 3–9 on the other overlapped hinge sides.

11 Glue the back of the entire piece to the curved surface of a ponytail hair clip, so the knots are exposed.

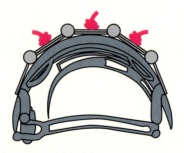

Use this as a key ring or as an embellishment to pants or a skirt. I especially like the flat connector pieces that add pattern to the chain. Simple geometry makes the look!

2½" SWIVEL LANYARD PULL

ELEVEN ⁵⁄₁₆ FLAT WASHERS

ELEVEN ⅛" QUICK LINK FASTENERS

GLUE

**1 ¼" KEY RING
(ANY SIZE WORKS)**

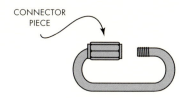

CONNECTOR PIECE

1 Open a quick link fastener by turning the connector piece as shown above.

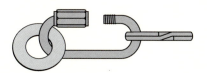

2 Thread a washer and the key ring onto the quick link. Turn the connector piece on the quick link closed.

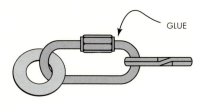

GLUE

3 To secure this connection, place a small drop of glue at the end of the connector piece.

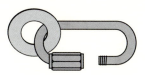

4 Open another quick link and thread a washer onto it.

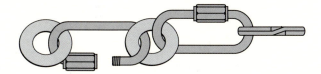

5 Thread the open quick link through the washer attached to the closed quick link. Pay attention to the direction in which you thread the quick link, as the location of the connector piece will determine the pattern in the chain. (In other words, if you choose to alternate the placement of the connector piece—as in the drawing—make sure you consistently alternate the direction as you add more links.)

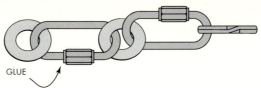

GLUE

6 To secure this connection, place a small drop of glue at the end of the connector piece on the quick link.

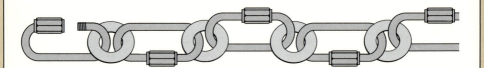

7 Repeat Steps 4–6 until you have used all of the washers. Keep the last quick link open.

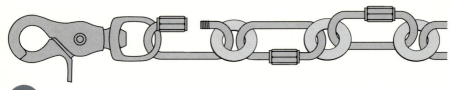

8 Thread the loop of the swivel lanyard pull through the open quick link. Close the quick link by turning the connector piece and secure the connection with glue.

This chain belt was inspired by the classic horse-bit connection by Gucci. I like how the clear tubing allows for the pointy screw to be visible without harming the wearer.

TOOLBOX

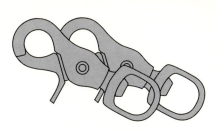

GLUE

**TWO 2½" SWIVEL
LANYARD PULLS**

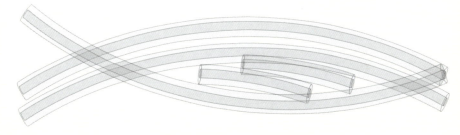

28" TRANSPARENT TUBING, ⅛" I.D. x ¼" O.D.

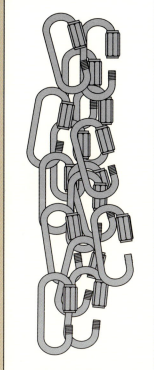

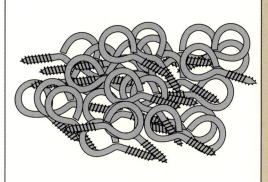

**TWENTY-EIGHT ⅛" x 1⅜"
SCREW EYES**

**FIFTEEN 18" QUICK LINK
FASTENERS**

**UTILITY
KNIFE**

RULER

INSTRUCTIONS

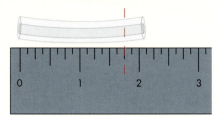

1 Cut the tubing into fourteen 1¾" segments by holding the tubing on a cutting surface (like a cutting mat or thick cardboard) next to a ruler and slicing the tube with a utility knife.

2 Holding one piece steady, put the threaded end of a screw eye into the hole of the tube and screw it in. Twist the screw eye as far into the tube as possible. Turn the piece over and twist another screw eye into the other side of the tube the same way. Repeat this step until you have made fourteen units.

CONNECTOR PIECE

3 Open a quick link by turning the connector piece on the side of the oval. Thread the quick link through a hole of a connected screw eye and tube piece.

GLUE

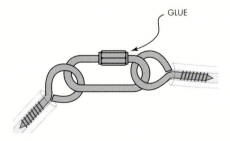

4 Thread another connected screw eye and tube piece onto the other side of the quick link before twisting the connector piece closed. To secure this connection, place a small drop of glue at the end of the connector piece.

5 Twist open another quick link and thread it through the free end of the connected screw eye and tube piece.

6 Repeat Steps 3–5 until you have completed the chain, being sure to leave an open quick link at either end.

7 At each end of the belt, attach a swivel lanyard pull by threading it onto the open quick link and twisting the connector shut. Place a drop of glue onto the connector piece to secure it.

8 To fasten the belt, wrap it around your waist or hips and connect one swivel lanyard pull end to a quick link in a comfortable place. Pick up the other end and hook that lanyard pull to another loop in the quick link, creating a loop.

QUICK LINK TUBE BELT

This double chain is simple, but the repeated S-hooks make it chunky and interesting. I wear it all the time because it matches everything.

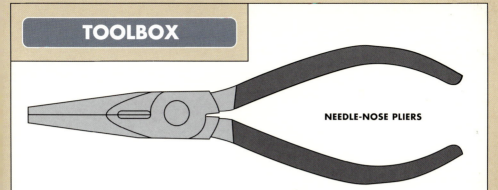

NEEDLE-NOSE PLIERS

THIRTY-THREE LARGE ($^{1.4}/_{10}$) JUMP RINGS

○

SMALL ($^1/_6$) JUMP RING

7mm SPRING RING

THIRTY-ONE CLOSED ZINC-PLATED S-HOOKS, SIZE 813 OR $^7/_8$"

INSTRUCTIONS

1 Twist open a large jump ring by holding one side steady with your fingers while turning the other side with a pair of pliers.

2 Thread the loop of the spring ring onto the open large jump ring.

3 Thread an S-hook onto the same large jump ring.

4 Twist the large jump ring closed.

5 Twist open another large jump ring and thread it through the other side of the S-hook.

6 Thread another S-hook through the open jump ring. Make sure it curves in the same direction as the first S-hook.

7 Twist the large jump ring closed.

8 Repeat Steps 5–7 until you have completed a chain of fourteen S-hooks. When you have attached the last S-hook, open a large jump ring and thread it through the end of the S-hook. Twist a small jump ring closed and thread it through the large open jump ring.

9 Twist the large jump ring closed.

10 Put this chain aside and begin a new chain. Start by twisting open a large jump ring and threading two S-hooks onto it. Then twist the jump ring closed. As with the first chain, make sure the S-hooks face the same direction.

11 Twist open another large jump ring and thread it through one of the attached S-hooks. Thread another S-hook through the opened jump ring, then twist the jump ring closed. Repeat until you have a chain of seventeen S-hooks.

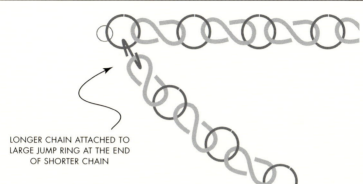

LONGER CHAIN ATTACHED TO LARGE JUMP RING AT THE END OF SHORTER CHAIN

12 Twist open a large jump ring and use it to connect an S-hook on the end of the longer chain to the large closed jump ring at the end of the shorter chain.

13 Twist the large jump ring closed.

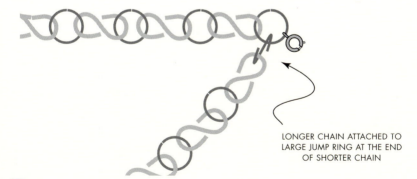

LONGER CHAIN ATTACHED TO LARGE JUMP RING AT THE END OF SHORTER CHAIN

14 Twist open another large jump ring and use it to connect the other end of the longer chain to the large jump ring on the other end of the shorter chain.

15 Twist the large jump ring closed.

DOUBLE CHAIN NECKLACE

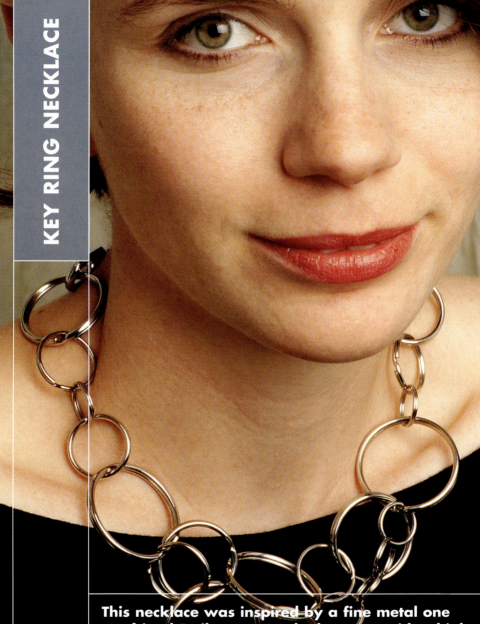

This necklace was inspired by a fine metal one my friend Emily wears. It looks great with a high-collared shirt, a low-cut scoop neck, or a button-up shirt that opens wide at the neck. The rings should sit against a plain background, allowing their connections to one another to speak for their fabulous selves.

TOOLBOX

THREE 1¼" KEY RINGS

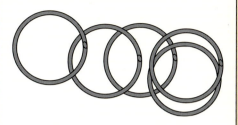

FIVE 1½" KEY RINGS

FOUR 1⅛" KEY RINGS

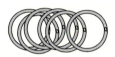

SIX ⅞" KEY RINGS

FIVE 1⅝" KEY RINGS

1⅜" x 2³/₁₆" SPRING CLIP, CHROME FINISH

INSTRUCTIONS

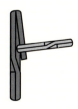

⅞" KEYRING

1½" KEYRING

1 Slip a ⅞" key ring onto the end of a 1½" key ring. (In other words, link the small key ring to the large key ring as if the smaller ring were a key.) **This is how all of the rings in the necklace connect to each other.**

KEY RING NECKLACE

2 Slip a 1⅛" key ring onto the 1½" key ring. Turn the rings until they are linked.

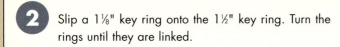
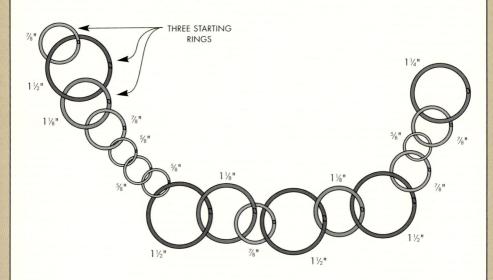

THREE STARTING RINGS

⅞"

1½"

1⅛"

⅞"

⅝"

⅝"

⅝"

1⅛"

1⅛"

1¼"

⅝"

⅞"

⅞"

1½"

1½"

⅞"

1½"

3 Continue to link the key rings to one another in the formation shown above.

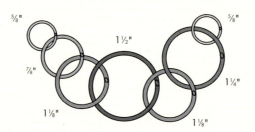

⅝"

⅝"

1½"

⅞"

1¼"

1⅛"

1⅛"

4 When that chain is complete, put it aside and begin a new chain connected as shown.

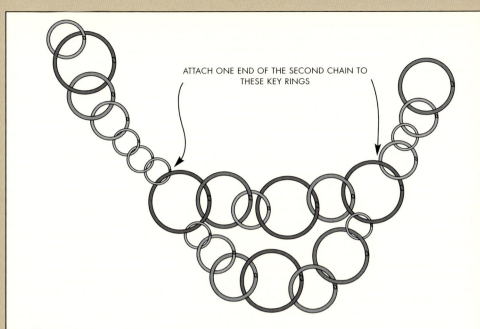

ATTACH ONE END OF THE SECOND CHAIN TO
THESE KEY RINGS

5 Attach the first chain to the second chain as shown above.

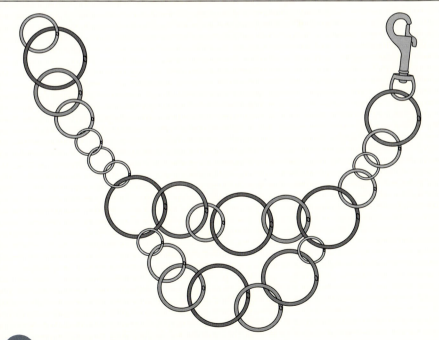

6 Slip the spring clip onto the 1¼" ring at the end of the chain.

This bracelet is interesting because the individual S-hooks are easily identifiable, but look quite different when presented side by side. The copper wire provides a nice contrast to the silvery S-hooks.

SIX CLOSED S-HOOKS, SIZE 809 OR 2"

14' 24-GAUGE COPPER WIRE

RULER

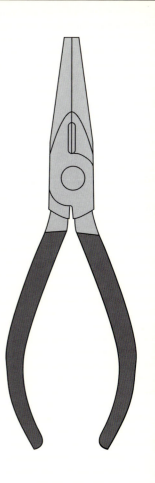

NEEDLE-NOSE PLIERS

INSTRUCTIONS

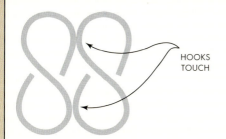

HOOKS TOUCH

1 Use the wire cutters in the middle of the pliers to cut two pieces of copper wire, each 12" long. Place two S-hooks side by side in a vertical orientation (see illustration at left), making sure they curve the same way. The hooks will touch each other at the top and bottom.

2 Wrap one of the cut wire pieces around both S-hooks where they touch at the top; use the whole length of the wire. Secure the end of the wire by bending the tip down slightly towards the rest of the wrapped wire (using the pliers), tucking the end of the wire under a wire that has already been wrapped, or tucking the end into the area between the two S-hooks.

3 Wrap the other cut piece of wire around both of the S-hooks where they touch at the bottom. Make sure the end of the wire doesn't protrude.

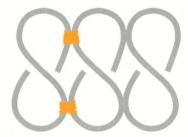

4 Cut two more 12" pieces of copper wire. Place another S-hook next to the first two in the same orientation.

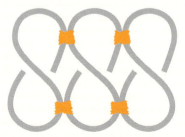

5 Wrap a piece of wire around the top and bottom areas where the S-hooks touch each other.

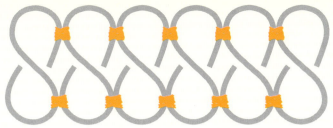

6 Repeat Steps 2–5 until all six S-hooks are connected.

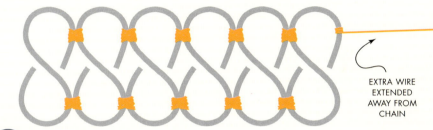

EXTRA WIRE
EXTENDED
AWAY FROM
CHAIN

7 Cut two more 12" pieces of copper wire. Choose an end of the S-hook chain on which to make a loop closure. Starting at the top, place the end of the wire inside the S-hook and wrap it around the edge three times, stopping with the excess wire extended away from the S-hook chain.

8 About ¼" away from the end of the S-hook, bend the wire back toward the chain to create a loop.

9 Wrap the wire around the S-hook on the far side of the loop three times.

10 Bend another loop in the wire like the first.

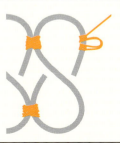

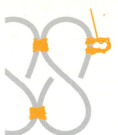

11 Wrap the wire once around the S-hook edge and make a third loop. Then wrap the wire around the S-hook twice.

12 Wrap the wire around all three looped pieces of wire to hold them together.

13 Continue to wrap the rest of the wire around the S-hook. Be sure to wrap the area on the inside of the loop as well. Make sure the end of the wire does not stick up. If you need to, bend it down or tuck the end under another piece of wire.

14 Repeat Steps 7–13 to make a second loop on the bottom of the S-hook.

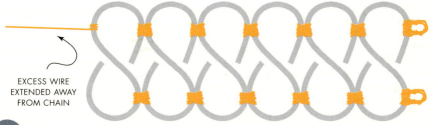

EXCESS WIRE
EXTENDED AWAY
FROM CHAIN

15 Cut two more 12" wire pieces. On the other side of the S-hook chain, place the end of a new piece of wire on the inside of the S-hook. Starting at the top, in the same direction as the wire connections, wrap the wire around the S-hook three times. Stop with the excess wire extended away from the S-hook chain.

16 About ¾" from the end of the S-hook, bend the wire straight back toward the S-hook chain and wrap the wire around the S-hook edge again. Here you can make an adjustment to the size of the bracelet to fit the wrist by lengthening the extended wire. (Keep in mind that half this length will form the hook of the bracelet.)

17 Bend the wire again so that another double length extends past the S-hook and wrap the wire around the S-hook edge again.

18 Extend a third piece of wire in the same way as the first two. Wrap the rest of the wire around the S-hook edge. Be sure that the end of the wire does not protrude.

SIDE VIEW

19 Using needle-nose pliers, pinch all three extended double pieces together. Treating this extension as one unit, bend it in half to create a hook closure.

20 Repeat Steps 15–19 on the bottom of the S-hook to make the bottom hook closure.

The edges of hexagon-shaped nuts fit together perfectly to create the pendant on this elegant necklace. Changing the color and length of the string are easy ways to personalize this piece. I like the way it looks when the pendant hangs right at the collarbone.

TOOLBOX

3 YARDS COLORED STRING, WAXED NYLON MENDING TWINE, EMBROIDERY FLOSS, OR CRAFT TWINE

ELEVEN SMALL (8-32) COARSE-THREAD HEX NUTS

SCISSORS

INSTRUCTIONS

1 Lay eleven small nuts in the configuration shown here.

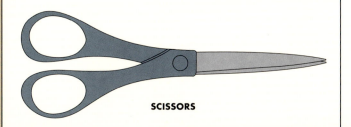

2 Cut a 4" piece of colored string. Starting with the bottom row, tie the two adjacent sides of the nut together with a square knot as shown. Pull tight and cross the strings again in the other direction, tucking one side over and around the other. Again, pull tight to secure the knot. After the knot has been tied tight, hold the ends of the string upright and cut the string as close to the knot as possible without cutting the knot.

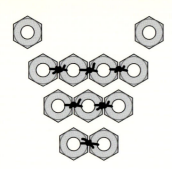

3 Cut five more 4" pieces of colored string. Moving across in straight rows, tie square knots between all of the nuts whose sides touch, using new string for each knot. Like the first knot, cut the excess string as close to the knot as possible without cutting the knot. Make sure you tie all the knots on the same side of the formation. This is the back of the pendant.

4 Cut twelve more 4" pieces of colored string. Starting with each of the two pieces in the top row, tie the nuts on the diagonal sides.

5 Move down to the next row, tying the nuts to each other on both diagonal sides. When you have completed this row, tie the next row on the diagonal sides. Make sure all sides that touch are tied together.

6 Flip the pendant over. The front side is now facing up.

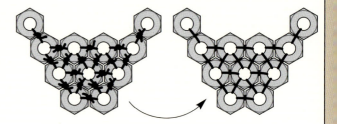

7 Cut two 36" pieces of colored string. Fold one of the pieces of string in half, then fold it in half again. Set aside the second piece of string.

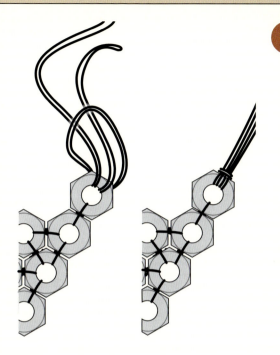

8 Thread the loop through one of the nuts at the top of the pendant, from the front to the back. Put your fingers through the middle of the loop (making sure they go through the center of both pieces) and grab all of the strings. Pull the strings though the loop and tighten. Gather the loose strings together and tie a knot at the end next to the nut. Cut the ends of the strings to even them.

9 Fold the second piece of string and bring the two ends together to make a loop. Repeat Step 8, threading the loop though the other nut on the top row. To wear the necklace, tie the ends together in a bow at the back of the neck at the desired length.

This is the necklace that started it all. I made it for my friend Frances and became thoroughly intrigued by the idea of making jewelry with materials from the hardware store. I particularly like the lightness and elegance of this necklace.

TOOLBOX

**36" NYLON-COATED MINIATURE WIRE,
7-STRAND (0.022" DIAMETER)**

**ELEVEN SMALL (8-32)
COARSE-THREAD HEX NUTS**

**SEVENTEEN
2mm CRIMP BEADS**

TWO SMALL (⅛) JUMP RINGS

7mm SPRING RING

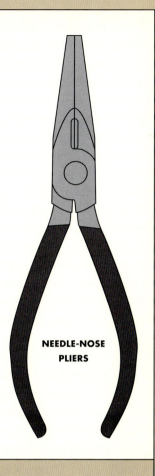

**NEEDLE-NOSE
PLIERS**

INSTRUCTIONS

1 Close a small jump ring by holding one side with your fingers and twisting the ends together with the pliers. Make sure that the ends of the ring touch so the thread will not pass through the side of the ring. Thread the jump ring onto the wire. Bring the ends of the wire together so the jump ring falls to the middle of the wire.

2 Thread both ends of the wire through a crimp bead, pushing the bead to about ⅛" from the jump ring to create a loop that captures the jump ring.

3 Using the needle-nose pliers, squeeze the bead to flatten it.

FLATTENED BEAD

4 Hold a nut between the two wires next to the crimped bead. The flat surface of the nut should be facing you so you can see through the hole.

5 Put one end of the cord through the hole, entering from the front.

6 Put the other end of the cord through the hole, entering from the back.

7 Thread both wires through another crimp bead and push down toward the nut. The second bead should be about 1" away from the first (with the nut between the two beads). Squeeze the crimp bead flat.

STRUNG BUT NOT FLATTENED

8 Repeat Steps 4–7 until you have reached the desired length. Do not crimp the last bead.

9 Twist open a jump ring and thread it through the loop of the spring ring. Twist the jump ring closed.

10 Thread the closed jump ring onto one of the wires at the end of the necklace.

11 Take the end of the wire with the jump ring and thread it back through the crimp bead, capturing the jump ring in a loop of wire. Squeeze the bead flat with needle-nose pliers.

12 Bend the straight wire away from the looped wire. Cut the straight wire as close to the crimped bead as possible without cutting through the looped wire. If the extra length of the looped wire is too long, cut it as close to the crimped bead as possible without cutting the loop.

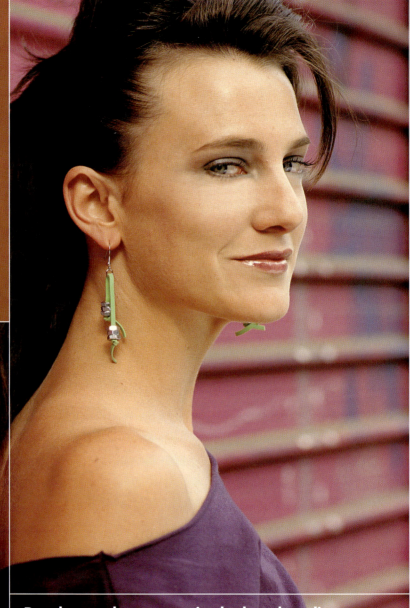

People are always surprised when they discover these earrings are made from rubber bands. I love the way the edges of the nuts catch the light as they dangle from the hooks, making the earrings sparkle. If you have trouble finding rubber bands in fun, bright colors at the hardware store, check out the stationery store.

TWO RUBBER BANDS IN THE SAME SIZE, THICKNESS, AND COLOR

TWO FRENCH EARRING WIRES

TWO SMALL (⅛) JUMP RINGS

TWELVE SMALL (8-32) COARSE THREAD HEX NUTS

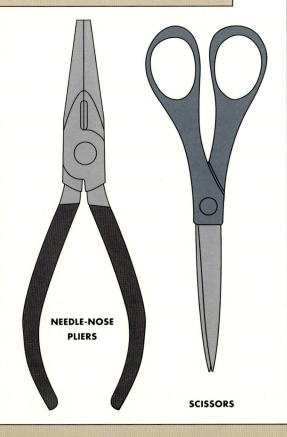

NEEDLE-NOSE PLIERS

SCISSORS

INSTRUCTIONS

1 Open a small jump ring by holding one side with your fingers and twisting the other side away from it with a pair of pliers.

OPEN JUMP RING

SIDE VIEW

2 Slip the closed circle of an earring wire through the open small jump ring.

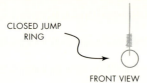

CLOSED JUMP RING

FRONT VIEW

3 Twist the end of the jump ring back together using your finger and a pair of pliers so the ends touch each other.

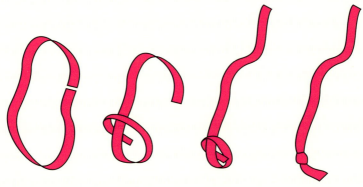

4 Cut a colored rubber band and tie a knot at one end by making a loop and pulling the end through.

5 String three nuts onto the rubber band, down to the knot.

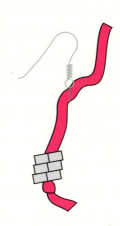

6 Thread the rubber band through the jump ring of the earring wire. The jump ring should fall at the middle of the rubber band.

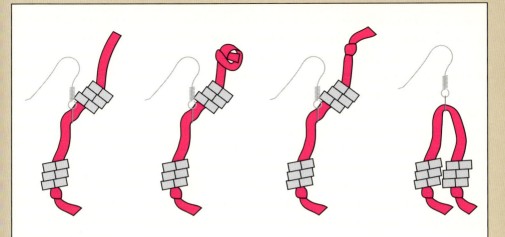

7 Thread three more nuts onto the rubber band. Tie a knot at the open end of the rubber band.

8 Repeat all steps to make a matching earring.

RUBBER BAND EARRINGS

Black and silver are always a crowd-pleasing combination. This necklace is elegant in its simplicity, and appeals to both guys and girls. If you wish to add more silver, add coupling nuts as beads to either side of the tied knots.

¼" **COUPLING NUT**

TWO 4.5mm FOLDOVER CORD ENDS

TWO SMALL (⅙) JUMP RINGS

7mm SPRING-RING

GLUE

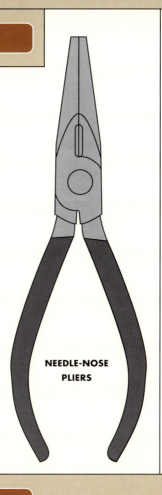

NEEDLE-NOSE PLIERS

48" CORD, ROPE OR LEATHER (SIZE 16 OR ³⁄₃₂")

INSTRUCTIONS

1 Cut two pieces of cord, each 24" long.

2 Thread a coupling nut onto both cords. Bring the ends of all four cords together so the coupling nut falls to the center.

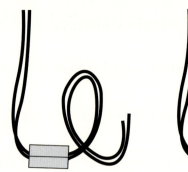

3 Holding the coupling nut in the center, tie a knot on one side by making a loop with the cords together and pulling the ends through the loop.

4 Tie a knot on the other side of the nut.

5 Measure the necklace around the neck to determine the desired length and cut the cords to that length.

6 On one side, place the ends of the cords into the cord ends and fold each metal flap over the ends with pliers. If you wish to make this connection even more secure, add a bit of glue to the inside of the cord end. Squeeze the metal flaps tight. Repeat on the other side of the necklace.

7 Twist open a jump ring by holding one side with your fingers and twisting the other side with a pair of pliers. Thread the jump ring through the hole of a cord end. Twist the jump ring closed.

8 Twist open another jump ring and thread it through the other cord end.

9 Thread the loop of a spring ring through the open jump ring. Twist the jump ring closed.

COUPLING NUT CHOKER

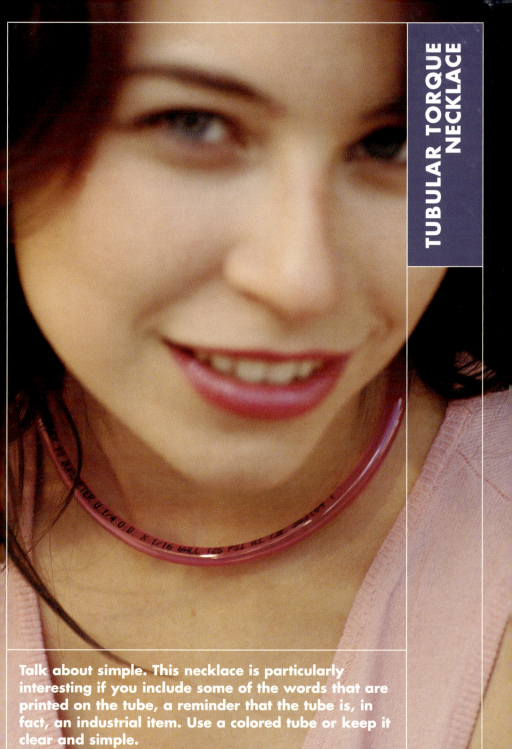

Talk about simple. This necklace is particularly interesting if you include some of the words that are printed on the tube, a reminder that the tube is, in fact, an industrial item. Use a colored tube or keep it clear and simple.

NECKLACE SHORTENER

TWO ZINC-PLATED
³⁄₁₆" x 1³⁄₁₆"
SCREW EYES, SIZE 210

14" PLASTIC TUBING
(¼" **O.D.** x ⅛" **I.D.**)

1 Measure the length of tube around your neck and cut to desired size.

2 Holding the tube steady, put the threaded end of a screw eye into the hole at the end of the tubing. Screw the screw eye into the tube by twisting the ring at the end. Be sure to screw it into the tubing as far as possible.

3 Twist the other screw eye into the other end of the tubing. The tubing should have a ring sticking out of each end.

CLOSED   OPEN

4 Open a necklace shortener by gently pulling on each side.

5 Put the necklace shortener into each screw eye and close to fasten around the neck.

CLEAR CHAIN BRACELET

People are often baffled by this bracelet—what is it made of? The chain adapts easily to a thin belt, a belly chain, a necklace, earrings, or a zipper pull.

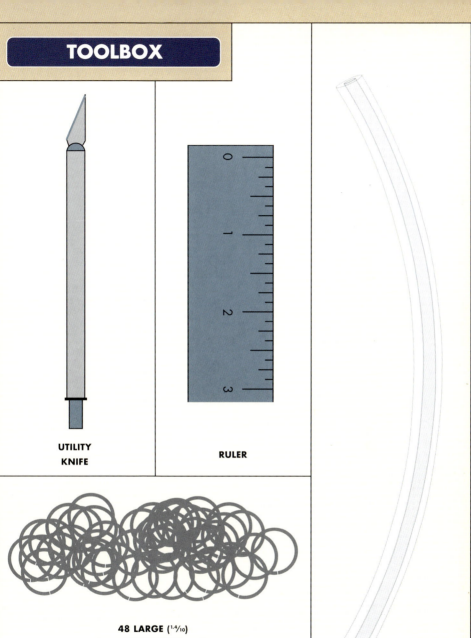

**UTILITY
KNIFE**

RULER

48 LARGE ($^{1 \cdot 4}/_{10}$)
JUMP RINGS

7mm SPRING RING

SMALL ($^{1}/_{6}$) **JUMP RING**

12" CLEAR PLASTIC TUBING
($^{3}/_{8}$" **O.D.** x $^{1}/_{4}$" **I.D.**)

CLEAR CHAIN BRACELET

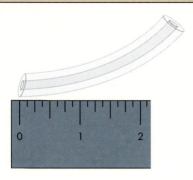

1 On a cutting surface (like a cutting mat or heavy cardboard), hold the end of the clear tubing to a ruler.

2 Cut ¼" pieces of the tubing using a utility knife. You may want to cut off several pieces of tubing at once. (The bracelet shown has forty-seven clear tube pieces.)

3 Open a large jump ring by holding one side of the ring with your fingers while twisting the other side away with the pliers.

4 Thread the loop of a spring ring through the open jump ring.

5 Slip a piece of the cut tubing through the open jump ring, then twist the jump ring closed.

6 Open another jump ring and slip it through the cut tubing.

7 Slip another tubing piece through the open jump ring. Then twist the jump ring closed.

8 Continue making this chain until you have reached the desired length.

9 End the chain with a closed large jump ring.

10 Twist open a small jump ring and thread it though the closed large jump ring. Twist the small jump ring closed.

11 Wrap the finished bracelet around your wrist and clasp the spring ring to the small jump ring to close it.

CLEAR CHAIN BRACELET

From a distance no one would ever guess this bracelet was made from electrical tape. If you are not satisfied with the electrical tape color selection, check out the duct tape.

½" x ½" VELCRO WITH ADHESIVE BACK

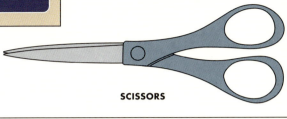

SCISSORS

¾"-WIDE PVC ELECTRICAL TAPE

FLEXIBLE MEASURING TAPE (OPTIONAL)

½" STRIP SCRAP PAPER (ABOUT 11" LONG)

INSTRUCTIONS

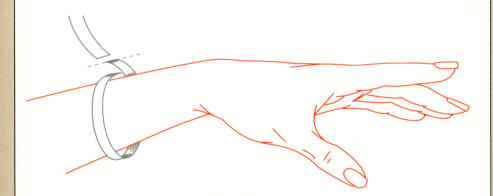

1 Wrap the paper around the wrist to measure bracelet size, adding an extra ½" to accommodate the Velcro closure. (You can also use a flexible tape measure.) Cut the paper to size and place it on a flat work surface.

2 Unpeel the tape from the roll and tape the end of the paper to the work surface. The roll should still be attached to the end of the tape and should be held directly above the strip of paper.

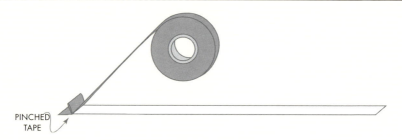

PINCHED
TAPE

3 Making sure that the tape has covered at least ½" of the paper, pinch the tape together, pressing it tightly, so that a small part of the tape sticks to itself.

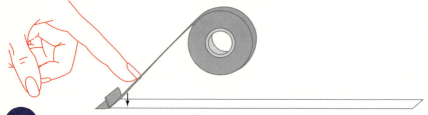

4 Adhere another ¼" or so of the tape to the paper by pressing down with your finger.

5 Pinch the tape again so that it sticks to itself. It does not matter how much you pinch; you may also want to try pinching it on a diagonal as a variation. If the tape goes off the paper, bend or stick it back so it covers the strip.

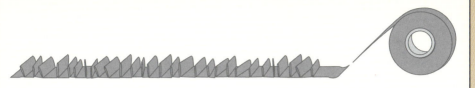

6 Continue pinching and pressing until the paper is entirely covered, leaving a flat area at the end of the bracelet. (It doesn't matter how many folds it takes to cover the paper, only that the paper is covered.) When you reach the end of the paper, cut the tape from the roll.

7 Peel up the tape and paper from the work surface and flip it over.

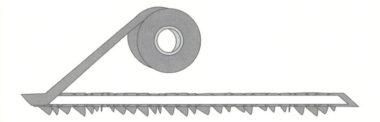

8 Starting from one end, adhere the tape to the back side. Be sure to cover the paper entirely, as well as the sticky side of the tape. Do not pull the tape too tightly as it stretches easily. Trim away any exposed sticky edges.

9 Put the bracelet back on the work surface, bumpy side up. Cut a ¼" x ¼" piece of Velcro.

TEXTURED TAPE BRACELET

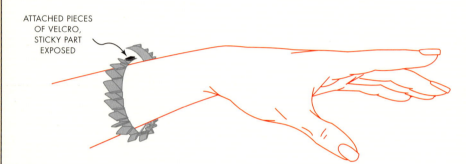

ATTACHED PIECES
OF VELCRO,
STICKY PART
EXPOSED

10 Keeping the two Velcro pieces attached to one another, peel the backing off of one side and stick it to the flat area at one end of the bracelet. Peel the backing from the other side of the Velcro so the sticky part on top is exposed.

ATTACHED PIECES
OF VELCRO,
STICKY PART
EXPOSED

11 Wrap the bracelet around the wrist, beginning with the Velcro end. As the bracelet encircles the wrist, the underside should just touch the sticky top of the Velcro.

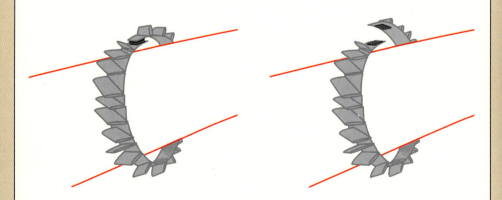

12 Open the bracelet by separating the Velcro sides from one another. Press the sticky back to the tape as firmly as possible.

I like this wristband because I enjoy creating geometric designs with tape. It is so simple, but has so many possibilities. There are lots of color options to match any outfit or personality.

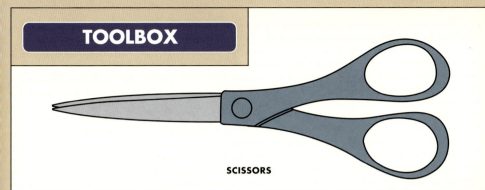

SCISSORS

**TWO DIFFERENT COLORS ¾"-WIDE
PVC ELECTRICAL TAPE**

FLEXIBLE MEASURING TAPE (OPTIONAL)

**VELCRO WITH
ADHESIVE BACK
(AT LEAST ¼" x 1")**

SCRAP PAPER (AT LEAST 9" x 1½")

INSTRUCTIONS

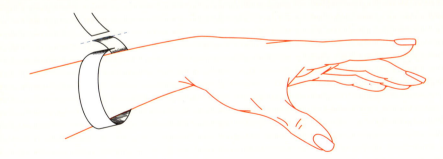

1 Wrap the paper around the wrist to determine wristband size, adding ½" to accommodate the Velcro closure. (You can also use a flexible tape measure.) Cut the paper to size and place it on a flat work surface.

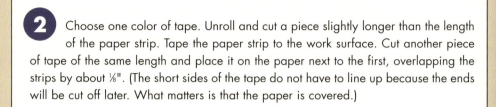

2 Choose one color of tape. Unroll and cut a piece slightly longer than the length of the paper strip. Tape the paper strip to the work surface. Cut another piece of tape of the same length and place it on the paper next to the first, overlapping the strips by about ⅛". (The short sides of the tape do not have to line up because the ends will be cut off later. What matters is that the paper is covered.)

3 Cover the entire paper with strips of tape. Make sure excess tape remains along the bottom edge.

4 Choose another color of tape and cut a piece about 4" long. With the scissors, cut the strip of tape in half lengthwise. Make different designs by cutting the new color along the length, on a curve, in a zigzag, or diagonally.

5 Stick these cut pieces on top of the wristband to create a design. (Don't worry about going over the edges.) Cut more pieces of different lengths and widths, sticking them to the wristband until you are satisfied with the design.

6 Unstick the wristband from the work surface and flip it over.

7 Using electrical tape in the original color, unroll and cut a piece slightly longer than the paper. Stick the tape to the length of the wristband's top back side.

8 Layer strips of tape, as you did on the front side, to cover all of the paper.

9 To make this wristband reversible, create another pattern on the back with the second color of electrical tape.

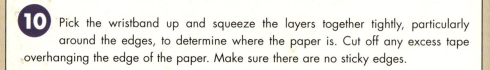

10 Pick the wristband up and squeeze the layers together tightly, particularly around the edges, to determine where the paper is. Cut off any excess tape overhanging the edge of the paper. Make sure there are no sticky edges.

11 Cut a ½" x 1½" piece of Velcro.

VELCRO PIECE
ATTACHED

12 Keeping the two Velcro pieces stuck together, peel the backing off of one piece and stick it to one end of the wristband.

VELCRO PIECE
WITH EXPOSED
STICKY SURFACE

13 Peel off the other side of the Velcro backing so the sticky surface is exposed. Wrap the wristband around the wrist so that it fits comfortably, allowing the side without the Velcro to touch the exposed sticky surface.

14 Open the wristband and press each side of the Velcro firmly into place.

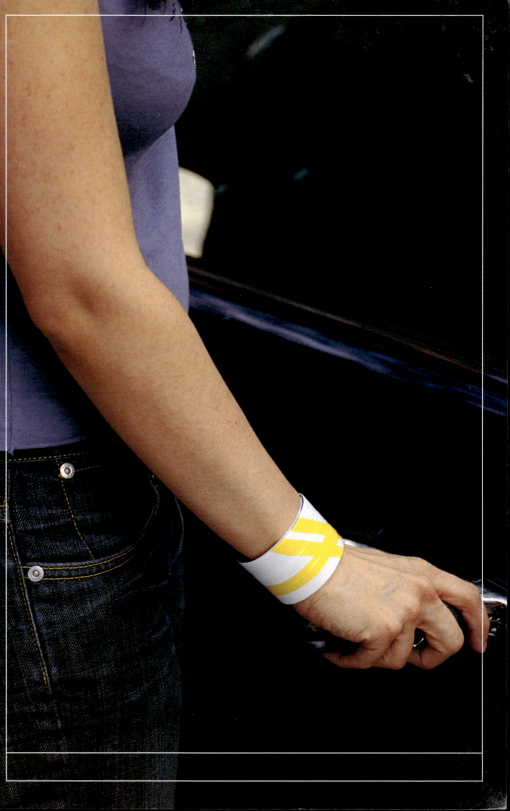

O-RING CELL PHONE CHARM

O-rings make light and bouncy charms on a cell phone. They also make it is easy to distinguish your cell phone from your friends'.

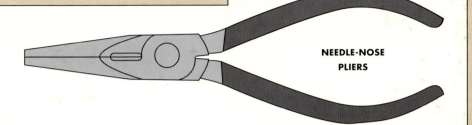

NEEDLE-NOSE
PLIERS

LARIAT FINDING

THREE #5 O-RINGS
(³⁄₈" O.D. x ¼" I.D. x ¹⁄₁₆")

THREE SMALL
(⅛) JUMP RINGS

INSTRUCTIONS

1 Twist open a small jump ring by holding one side with your fingers and twisting the other side with a pair of needle-nose pliers.

2 Thread two O-rings onto the open jump ring.

3 Twist the jump ring closed by using your fingers on one side and twisting the other side with the pliers.

4 Twist open a second jump ring and thread it through one of the attached O-rings.

5 Thread another O-ring through the opened jump ring. Twist the jump ring closed.

6 Twist open a third jump ring. Thread it through an attached O-ring.

7 Thread the metal ring of a lariat finding through the open jump ring. Twist the jump ring closed.

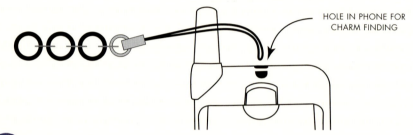

HOLE IN PHONE FOR
CHARM FINDING

8 To attach the charm to the phone, pinch the loop of the lariat finding and push it through the small hole on the phone, then bring the charm through the loop and pull it tight.

I like to make these bracelets in different O-ring sizes and wear a few at the same time. They are decorative without being heavy or awkward. These bracelets are easy to make and, with no closure, are easy to put on and take off.

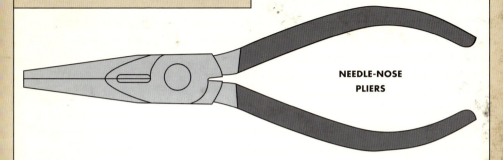

NEEDLE-NOSE PLIERS

SIX LARGE (¹·⁴⁄₁₀) JUMP RINGS

SIX #27 O-RINGS
(1⅛" O.D. x ⅞" I.D. x ⅛")

INSTRUCTIONS

1 Twist open a large jump ring by holding one side with your fingers and twisting the other side with a pair of needle-nose pliers.

2 Thread two O-rings onto the open jump ring.

3 Twist the jump ring closed by holding on to one side with your fingers and turning the other side with the pliers.

4 Twist open another large jump ring. Thread it onto one of the attached O-rings. Thread another O-ring onto the jump ring and twist the jump ring closed.

5 Continue to attach O-rings to jump rings until you run out of O-rings. To finish, attach the beginning of the chain to the end with the last jump ring, making sure that the rings stay flat and do not twist. To wear the bracelet, just stretch it over your hand.

GLOSSARY

The following is a listing of all the items used in this book. It is divided into two sections, one for supplies traditionally found in hardware stores and one for supplies traditionally found in craft, bead, and jewelry-making stores.

When you start shopping for your hardware, remember that all hardware stores are organized a little differently. Usually the larger chain stores (the kinds that sell everything from eye screws to outdoor furniture) have a designated "hardware" department, where you can find most of the supplies needed for the projects in this book. Smaller, more traditional stores may stock their hardware in different areas, even behind the counter in unmarked bins. If you don't see what you need, ask for help.

HARDWARE STORE

COPPER WIRE

This type of wire is a great conductor for electricity and is often used for wiring appliances. It is good for jewelry-making because it is easy to bend and is an attractive natural orange color.

Wire is measured in gauges, determined by its circumference. The higher the gauge number, the thinner the wire. Since copper wire is flexible, even the thicker kind is easy to use for jewelry.

WHERE TO FIND: WIRE OR ELECTRICAL SECTION

COUPLING NUT

Coupling nuts are used to connect rods to one another. They can also be used as spacers, separating two objects the distance of the coupling nut. A coupling nut looks like a large, hexagon-shaped, silver bead and is perfect for jewelry.

Coupling nuts are often differentiated by three numbers. The first is the diameter, the second is the amount of threads per inch (tpi), and the third is the length. The coupling nuts used in this book are size ½" x 20 x ⅞". Any size below a ¼" diameter is referred to in standard numbers rather than by length.

WHERE TO FIND: NUTS AND BOLTS SECTION

ELECTRICAL TAPE

This flame-retardant tape is used to insulate wire splices. Smooth and flexible with weak adhesive (and therefore more manageable than other tapes), electrical tape adapts well to jewelry-making.

Electrical tape comes in a few different widths but ¾" is the most common.

WHERE TO FIND: ELECTRICAL SUPPLY SECTION, NEAR WIRES, LIGHTING FIXTURES, AND PLUGS

GLUE

There are many different types of glue for different applications. Read package directions to determine if a particular glue will adhere to the material with which you are working.

Strong general glues like KrazyGlue, Epoxi, or Duco Cement will work for all of the projects in this book.

WHERE TO FIND: WITH ADHESIVES OR GENERAL-PURPOSE ITEMS

HEX NUT

Hex nuts, named for their hexagonal shape, are often paired with bolts to capture material on either side of a metal shaft. Nuts are great for jewelry because of their interesting shape and large hole. However, they can get heavy quickly, so use small sizes and/or limit the number you use in one piece of jewelry.

Nuts are differentiated by two numbers. The first is the diameter of the nut and the second is the amount of threads per inch (tpi). A nut marked 8-32 (which is the size used for the projects in this book) has an inside diameter designated by the number 8 and has a tpi of 32. Any nut that is smaller than ¼" is referred to by a standard numbering system rather than an actual measurement (such as 8).

WHERE TO FIND: NUTS AND BOLTS SECTION

KEY RING

A key ring is a circular connector that does not easily release the connected object (such as a key). They are useful in jewelry-making because they can link to each other or other objects.

Key rings are sold according to the size of their outside diameter.

WHERE TO FIND: LOCKSMITH AND KEY-CUTTING AREA

L-BRACKET

L-brackets (also called angle braces or plates, or corner brackets) are traditionally used to strengthen and support joints and corners of things like shelves and picture frames. It is better to use small L-brackets for jewelry-making since they can get heavy.

These brackets are generally labeled with two measurements: the first is the length of one side, the second is the flat area that makes the L shape. For example, if an L-bracket is labeled 1" x $\frac{3}{8}$", it is 1" long and has a surface that is $\frac{3}{8}$" wide.

WHERE TO FIND: BRACES AND BRACKETS SECTION, NEAR THE HINGES

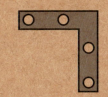

MATCHES

Use matches to melt nylon plies of rope together so they won't fray. You can also use a ligher.

WHERE TO FIND: NEAR THE BARBECUE OR TOBACCO SECTION, OFTEN AT THE FRONT BY THE REGISTER.

NEEDLE-NOSE PLIERS

This multipurpose tool is used to grab and squeeze objects that are too small or awkwardly placed to be manipulated with the fingers. Most needle-nose pliers include wire cutters just above the hinge.

Needle-nose pliers are great for small applications, particularly when bending wire into a small loop.

WHERE TO FIND: HAND TOOL SECTION OR BEHIND THE REGISTER. YOU CAN ALSO FIND THIS TOOL IN CRAFT, JEWELRY-MAKING, AND BEAD STORES.

WIRE CUTTERS

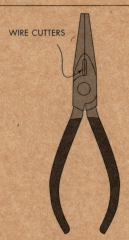

NYLON ROPE

Nylon rope is made from multiple plies of nylon string. It comes in many colors and sizes, giving you many options to choose from. Neon-colored nylon rope, traditionally used for masonry, chalk lines, duck decoys, and fishing net repair, is great for making a bold statement with jewelry.

Rope is measured using its own gauge system: the bigger the number, the smaller the diameter. The Loop Rope Wire Bracelet (page 42) uses number 3½ or ⁷⁄₆₄". The Neon Rope Earrings (page 46) use number 18 rope.

WHERE TO FIND: FISHING OR ROPE SECTION

O-RING

These black rubber rings are commonly used in plumbing. They work well for jewelry-making because they are light, flexible, and waterproof.

O-rings have their own standard numbering system: the higher the number, the bigger the ring. Sometimes the inside and outside diameters (I.D. and O.D) are also given.

WHERE TO FIND: PLUMBING SUPPLY SECTION

PLASTIC TUBING

Plastic tubing is used to carry fluid from one place to another. Transparent tubing becomes an interesting design element in jewelry-making; colored tubing can be challenging to find but it is worth the effort.

Tubing is measured by the inside diameter (I.D.) and outside diameter (O.D.). Make sure you have the correct I.D. for your application. (In other words, to secure a screw eye into the end of the tube, make sure that the I.D. is small enough for the threads of the screw to grab onto the wall of the tubing.)

WHERE TO FIND: PLUMBING OR TUBING AREA, OR WHEREVER RACKS OF MATERIALS ARE SOLD BY THE FOOT.

QUICK LINK

Quick links (also known as [ ] ed connectors) are used to connect one thing to another, such as a [ ] screw eyes in the ceiling. Quick links are great for jewelry bec[ ]se [ ]e connector piece creates a pattern when repeated.

Quick links are measured b[ ] ne [ ]iameter of the oval rod. For example, a ⅛" (3.5mm) quick link ha[ ] r[ ] that is ⅛" thick.

WHERE TO FIND: WITH OTHER H[ ] CLIPS, AND LINKS, OR SOMETIMES WITH THE ROPE AND CHAIN SPOOLS

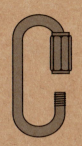

RUBBER BAND

Rubber bands can add col[ ] bounce to jewelry. If you are not satisfied with the color sele[ ] the hardware store, look for more variety at a stationery store.

WHERE TO FIND: WITH GENERA[ ] SE ITEMS

RUBBER SHEETING

Rubber sheeting is used as cu[ ] or seal between two items, such as the top and bottom of a jam j[ ]

Rubber sheeting is sold in a s[ ]" ackage or in loose pieces, and is available in different thicknesse[ ] most useful for these projects range from 1/16" to ⅛" thick. If you ca[ ]ot [ ]d individual sheets, consider buying a vacuum cleaner belt, wh[ ] a ring of rubber sheeting. It most commonly comes in red or bl[ ] [ ]t you might be able to find it in another color depending on the [ ]tore you are in.

WHERE TO FIND: OFTEN IN THE PL[ ] SECTION

S-HOOKS

S-hooks are used to quickly co[ ] hains or hanging objects to one another. Their simple shape is g[ ]t f[ ] creating patterns in jewelry.

S-hooks are either measured by t[ ] [ ]gth or by a standard numbering system. The Wide S-Hook Brac[ ]t ([ ]age 72), uses a #810 S-hook, which is 2" long. For the Doub[ ] [ ] in Necklace (page 64), use a #813, which is ⅞" long.

WHERE TO FIND: HANGING HARDW[ ]E S[ ]TION

SCISSORS

Scissors are handy for cutting mostly flat, thin material, like paper, rubber, and thread. Round or thick objects are more easily cut with a knife.

WHERE TO FIND: SCISSOR SECTION OR WITH GENERAL-PURPOSE ITEMS

SCREW EYE

Screw eyes (also known as eye hook screws) are used to hang objects and to hook things together. I like to combine screw eyes with plastic tubes for jewelry. When doing this, it is important to make sure the diameter of the screw is big enough to catch the material of the tube wall so it will remain attached.

Screw eyes are usually measured according to their height or the diameter of the screw. Sometimes they are assigned a number that represents their size.

WHERE TO FIND: WITH HOOKS AND OTHER HANGING HARDWARE

SPRING BOLT SNAP

A spring bolt snap provides a quick and temporary connection. The sliding part of this snap is called a bolt. This piece is good for jewelry because it is large enough to make a statement bolder than other jewelry fasteners, but it comes in sizes small enough to be worn.

Spring bolt snaps are labeled according to their length and sometimes width.

WHERE TO FIND: WITH OTHER HOOKS, CLIPS, AND LINKS

SWIVEL LANYARD PULL

A swivel lanyard pull (also called a trigger snap or snap hook) also provides a quick and temporary connection, but it is more secure than a spring bolt snap because both sides of the clasp head are curved.

Swivel lanyard pulls are measured according to their length and sometimes width.

WHERE TO FIND: WITH OTHER HOOKS, CLIPS, AND LINKS

VELCRO

Velcro is a kind of two-part tape: one part has tiny hooks on it and the other has tiny loops. When the two are pressed together, they stick. Velcro makes a great, clean closure for casual jewelry.

Velcro is sold in a variety of sizes and shapes and can be easily cut to the size desired. Be sure to buy Velcro with adhesive on the back, and be sure to match a hook piece to a loop piece.

WHERE TO FIND: ADHESIVE OR GENERAL-PURPOSE SECTION

WASHERS

Washers are used with screws to help distribute pressure over a greater surface area. Washers are great for jewelry because of their shape. When designing a piece of jewelry with washers, remember that the more or larger washers you use, the heavier the piece will be. Big washers (1" or larger) are good for belts while small washers (smaller than 1") work well for earrings and necklaces.

Washers are measured according to the inside and outside diameters (I.D. and O.D.). The I.D. refers to the size screw that can fit through the center of the washer. Washers with an I.D. smaller then ¼" are referred to by a numbering system.

WHERE TO FIND: WASHER SECTION, OR WITH OTHER ITEMS PACKAGED IN MASS QUANTITIES; OFTEN STOCKED NEAR THE SCREWS AND NUTS

CRAFT STORE

CHOKER CLAMP

A choker clamp (sometimes called a necklace clamp) puts a clean finish on the end of a ribbon or other wide strip of material. It also provides a loop at the end to attach a closure. Choker clamps are usually measured in millimeters.

CORD END

A cord end puts a clean finish on the ends of cords. It also provides a loop to attach a closure. Cord ends come in different sizes, determined by the size of the cord being finished.

CRIMPING BEAD

A crimping bead holds wire and cord in place. It is particularly useful with material that cannot be tied off (like nylon-coated wire). These beads are measured in millimeters. For the projects in this book, the exact size doesn't matter as long as a few pieces of the wire or cord fit through the hole before you squeeze it together.

EMBROIDERY FLOSS

Embroidery floss is a multi-plied thread that adds a nice, bold color to jewelry.

FLEXIBLE MEASURING TAPE

A flexible measuring tape is useful for measuring curved objects, like your wrist or waist.

FRENCH BARRETTE (Ponytail)

A French barrette (ponytail) is a curved metal structure that holds ponytails in place. It also has a good surface for gluing on decorations.

JUMP RINGS

CLOSED
TOP
VIEW

OPEN
TOP
VIEW

CLOSED
SIDE
VIEW

A jump ring is a simple wire ring used to connect and attach various jewelry parts. Jump rings are referred to by fractions (e.g., $^{1.4}/_{10}$). The first number represents the diameter of the wire in millimeters and the second number represents the diameter of the entire ring in millimeters.

To open a jump ring, hold one side of the ring with your fingers while twisting the other side away with needle-nose pliers.

LANYARD HOOK

A lanyard hook is a small clip that stays closed. In addition to a jewelry store, lanyard hooks can also be found at the end of a toilet chain in the plumbing section of the hardware store. They are measured in millimeters by length.

LARIAT FINDING

A lariat finding has a cord loop that is used to attach the finding to the side of a cell phone. It can also be attached to the end of a zipper or lanyard hole, or even a key ring or camera—any place with a small hole.

LOBSTER CLASP

A lobster clasp is a traditional jewelry clasp that has an oval shape similar to a lobster's claw. It is usually measured according to the overall length.

NECKLACE SHORTENER

A necklace shortener doubles over a long necklace and clips it together at a shorter length.

NYLON-COATED WIRE

Nylon-coated wire has a protective coating that makes it durable and water-resistant. It is sized in gauges: the larger the gauge number, the thicker the wire.

SPRING RING CLASP

A spring ring clasp is the most common jewelry clasp. Its size is determined by the diameter of the ring and is measured in millimeters.

SUPPLY SOURCES

All of the materials needed for the projects in this book should be easy to locate. If you are having trouble finding them in your local hardware and craft stores, try these websites.

HARDWARE

www.mcmaster.com
www.smallparts.com
www.thehomedepot.com
www.acehardware.com
www.lowes.com

JEWELRY FINDINGS

www.rings-things.com
www.firemoutaingems.com
www.riogrande.com
www.michaels.com

ACKNOWLEDGEMENTS

It is incredible to have the opportunity to thank in writing those who have lent me a hand, given me their time, and passed me some of their knowledge for this project and for all else I experience. Thanks to the 'rents, Robie and Fred, for endless help and support with everything, including my strange fashion sense and blue hair. Thank you Frances Lachowicz, who owns and wears my very first pair of earrings. Thanks to David-Siren Eisner, Miya Hideshima, and Theresa Kinsella for extraordinary support and advice. To Julie Sandy and her mom, Beverly Norton, for (most importantly) always being creative, talking me through my silly worries, looking out for me and, oh yeah, for help with research on this project. Thank you Raddy Ramos for scientific research and general good times. For other advice and information, thanks to friends I am lucky to work with everyday: Camilla Slattery (Bean's agent, among other things), Angel Rios, Duncan Gillis, and Larry Ona. For help with the photo shoot, thanks go to Marianne Rafter, Brooke Jacobs, Laly Zambrana, Teva Durham, and Amanda Brown. For their time, patience, and beautiful features, I'd like to thank the models: Emily FitzGerald, Lisa Gallagher, Julie Sandy, Todd Coleman, Matt Spaeth, Gelya Robb, Alexandra Levin, and Bean. I cannot thank Galen Smith enough for his genuine excitement with this project, his willingness to offer his time to the book (despite his ridiculous schedule), and, most importantly, for humoring me with discussions about the graphic possibilities and direction for *Hardwear*. I owe many thanks to Carl Williamson as well, for his time and dedication to making sure this book came out perfectly. And my final and huge THANK YOU goes out to Melanie Falick for making this work, for guiding me through the process, and for trusting my vision. I really appreciate it.

Marianne Rafter is a portrait, lifestyle, and fine art photographer based in New York. Her photographs have appeared in numerous publications, including the *New York Times, Town & Country, Glamour,* and *Graphis,* and are included in private collections in Europe and North America.